Microaggression

Then & Now

Creative Talents Unleashed

Anthologies Published by Creative Talents Unleashed

Cupid's Arrow

I Have a Name

Down The Rabbit Hole

Poetic Shadows – Ink and the Sword

Imperfect Paths

Shades of the Same Skin

Poetic Melodies

Divided Lines – A Poet's Stance

Writing Tips – Exploring the Writer's Path

Unleashed

Love, a Four Letter Word

GENERAL INFORMATION

Microaggression Then & Now

By

Creative Talents Unleashed

1st Edition: 2018

This Publishing is protected under Copyright Law as a "Collection". All rights for all submissions are retained by the Individual Author and or Artist. No part of this publishing may be Reproduced, Transferred in any manner without the prior **WRITTEN CONSENT** of the "Material Owner" or its Representative Creative Talents Unleashed.

www.ctupublishinggroup.com

Publisher Information
1st Edition: Creative Talents Unleashed
info@ctupublishinggroup.com

This Collection is protected under U.S. and International Copyright laws

Copyright © 2018: Creative Talents Unleashed

ISBN-13: 978-1-945791-50-5 (Creative Talents Unleashed)

Credits

Book Cover
Raja Williams

Editor
All Authors Responsible For Own Work

Foreword
Don Beukes

Foreword

In this new hard hitting anthology by *Creative Talents Unleashed*, authors from around the world pour out their experiences of 'Microaggression'.

The Merriam-Webster dictionary defines it as *"A comment or action subtly and often unconsciously expressing a prejudiced attitude towards a member of marginalized group"*

Derald Wing Sue defines Microaggression as " The brief and commonplace daily verbal, behavioral and environmental indignities, whether intentional or unintentional, that communicate hostile, derogatory, or negative racial, gender, and sexual orientation, and religious slights and insults to the target person or group"

In today's society we are all a part of, whether we like it or not; we are forever scrutinizing our dialogue and conversation, looking out for offensive and insulting content. Today, words don't just insult, they also inflict verbal violence with long lasting psychological effects, causing unimaginable inner conflict and problems with forming healthy personal relationships.

The authors of *Microaggression – Then & Now* are speaking out. They are victims themselves and bravely share their experiences, concerns, hopes and fears through poetry and prose. They speak of a lack of empathy and tolerance in society. They warn of how words can cut, stir, disrupt and destroy. They refuse to accept others telling you that 'you can't or 'you're not good enough'. They document long term derision, mocking of a person's skin color, sexual orientation and the dismissal of others and the lasting effects this has on all of us experiencing this. They want you to know that your handicap does not make you less of a human being. They know and understand that some of you struggle to find your voice and prefer to exist in the margins of society. They also realize that some of you wear your hearts on your sleeves and they want you to know that it is fine. It is what makes you unique. If others see this as a weakness or handicap, remain steadfast within yourself and take comfort in the knowledge that they themselves are the lost ones, the lonely ones, the broken ones.

Some of us unfortunately do not know which emotional tools to use to control our inner well-being, so when others silence us, overpower us, misunderstand us or dismiss us, we choose to step back behind our veil of inner personal safety. This anthology aims to give you the courage to speak out, reach out, and break the mold of silence.

Derald Wing Sue further argues that *"perpetrators of Microaggression are often unaware of the indignities that they inflict on others"*.

Be brave and find your voice to let them know that you refuse to be silent, you refuse to let them break you, you refuse to let them belittle you and dehumanize you. The authors in this anthology want you to know you are not alone.

Don Beukes, author of *The Salamander Chronicles*

Table of Contents

Foreword *Don Beukes*	v
Microaggression *Xavier Smith*	1
Acclimation *Michael Griffith*	2
Absence *Alicia Minjarez Ramirez*	3
Simple Minded People *Jeff Oliver*	4
The Tolerance of Intolerance *Justin R. Hart*	6
Is It Just Me *John Walker*	8
60 seconds *Jaz*	9
They *Vee Townsend*	10
The Rest is Silence *Ann Christine Tabaka*	11

A Sham *Susan O'Reilly*	12
Micro-aggression is… *J. Mulcahy-King*	13
Motherly Love *Lynn White*	14
My Handicap *Tammy S. Thomas*	15
Coloured *Bevan Boggenpoel*	16
The Necessities of Dark and Light *John Walker*	17
Vanishing Gardens *Baidha Fercoq*	18
Words *Markus Fleischmann*	19
Mansplain *Adam Levon Brown*	21
Stressing *Veronica "Vee" Thornton*	22
Heart's Reflection *Shelly Ambrose*	23
So Pretty *Maggie Mae*	24

The War Cry of Natives *William Wright, Jr.*	25
Embarrassment *Heath Brougher*	26
Personal *Shelly Buttenhoff Miller*	27
Collateral Damage *Vincent Van Ross*	28
Final Depressive Episode *Darrell Herbert*	29
In All Walks of Life *Mark Andrew Heathcote*	30
Microaggression: A Fabricated Reality *Xavier Smith*	31
Mirror of Hope *Monsif Beroual*	32
The Warrior Takes Her Place *Vee Townsend*	33
Broken *Ann Christine Tabaka*	35
My Worst Enemy *Vee Townsend*	36
Between the Eyes *Miriam Ruano*	37

This is a Choice *Ezekiel O Tracy*	39
Leper Apothecary *J. Mulcahy-King*	41
Promotion *Daginne Aignend*	42
Nation in Reparation *Bevan Boggenpoel*	43
The F*cking Bus Seat Saga *Zoe Maynard*	44
Black Smells *Daginne Aignend*	45
Subtle Aggression *Bevan Boggenpoel*	46
Whistle *Zoe Maynard*	47
Swept Aside *Baidha Fercoq*	49
Let Go *Shelly Ambrose*	50
Raised On Cartoons *Heath Brougher*	51
Who Are You? *Paige Turner*	52

The Micro Female *Brenda-Lee Ranta*	53
Diary of a Coloured Boy *Don Beukes*	54
Uncomfortable Question *John Walker*	55
Monks Swimming *Jim Lewis*	56
Why Am I Angry *Terika McQuinn*	59
Personal Experience *John Walker*	60
Words Can Hurt *Markus Fleischmann*	61
The Restaurant *Don Beukes*	62
Coco Sonya *Rusty Shuping*	64
Good Deeds that Turn Out the Other Way *Vincent Van Ross*	65
Luck or Blessing *Rusty Shuping*	66
Things I have Heard Said *Mark Andrew Heathcote*	67

The Beach *Don Beukes*	68
It's all Perspective *Rusty Shuping*	70
There is No Micro in Aggression *Brenda-Lee Ranta*	71
The Starving Artist Fund	74
CTU Connections	76

Microaggression

The sensitive mind is powerful
It champions empathy
It perfectly models sympathy
It offers grace
so abundantly
It accepts criticism and misspoken words
Ever so gracefully

The oversensitive mind is weak
It seeks to bury free speech
As deeply as a hidden treasure at sea
It weaponizes sympathy
To make another feel weak
It is absent of power
But instead abundant with malice

Xavier Smith

Acclimation

Have I changed for you,
a better fit, a better fate?

Have you changed for me,
a bitter taste now a better taste?

Do we absorb and expand
or do we retract and regroup?

Melting pot never quite hot enough
or never stirred in the right ways
for all spices to become flavors.

Dance and swirl, centrifuge of life
a music we only sense, never really hear,
never quite get those words out right.

Mix, stir, many-to-one
yet alone at day's end
in skins our own unique shade.

Stripes, spots, splotches, clean as ivory and teeth
beautiful as any trophy and kept as pure
as the dance will allow.

Do I move to your rhythm
or do you come for my words?

Do I misshape you to my desire
or do you mold me to your will?

Michael Griffith

Absence

You left
Like rain
After destroying
The bare countryside.

Below the leaves
Your name
Flying with the wind
Foreseen the verse,
Its useless tessitura
Upon the unpropitious
Yesterday.

I still don't understand
The seven letters
Building
Your absence.

It's not dark yet…
And the language
Of the sun
Is no longer the same.

Alicia Minjarez Ramirez

Translated by: *Alaric Gutiérrez*

Simple Minded People

Prejudice it happens among the same color
Hate
Why can't we love another?
Pain
A pointless separation
Race
A pointless assumption
Insane
Is what we are

Simple minded people
Make simple minded assumptions
And come to simple minded conclusions

A war on our skin
Where nobody wins
There's color in the crown
A king of nothing
Can you see the sin?
Who's gonna win?
When we all go home...

Why do you hate me?
I'm just like you...
My heart beats...just like you
The only difference
Is the color on the outside
Nothing is different
Deep down inside

Simple minded people
Make simple minded assumptions
And come to simple minded conclusions

Prejudice…
Pain…
Hate…
Rage...
Insane... is what we are

We need a change.

Jeff Oliver

The Tolerance of Intolerance

Can we feel the intimidation,
the perilous fear,
the hasty conclusions?
Do we fairly judge,
assume before knowing?
Can there be balance, blending
a rainbow of opportunity?
Do we see the results
from our desperate violence?
Is this the nature of our nature?

It is our irrational attitude,
our blatant bias
that creates this blind vision,
a short sided intolerance,
and narrow-mindedness.
Can we hear the bark
of the dogmatic bigot
left standing on the street?
Do we smell the trifling disregard,
the preconceived judgment,
the half-baked ignorance?

Can we taste the bitterness
of our personal choices?
Do we quench our thirst
with savory apprehension
and smell our pungent suspicions.
We feel our quick decisions,
then hear mocking disrespect,
and jeers for our fears.

We have had years of tears,
flooding our rivers
to sea...With color blindness,
Rainbows do blend!!!

Justin R. Hart

Is It Just Me

Microaggression
Often hard to glean
It's like passive-aggression
The intent is rarely seen
Was that an insult
Or is it just me
Do I just imagine
Oversensitivity
I get so confused
And feel quite unsure
Do you really care
Or are you pure unpure
Please be clear with me
Even if I'm pained
I'd rather know the ignorance
That flows inside your veins

John Walker

60 seconds

She said
"Ooh girl you look good!"
And then slid in a backhand of
"Showing off and all"
It knocked the wind out of my sails that had fought
to spread through a long journey to wellness and self-love
Somewhere in those silent seconds
I found my voice on its' way to the floor
And though it was only a whisper
I stood in my worth to declare
"I am celebrating my freedom"
She backed off
to immediately retract her micro-aggression
with some type of plastic flowery compliment cover-up
With an offer of sugar
to wash down the bitter
she delivered just a second before
I remembered by wings
I stepped forward past her shadows
and walked unapologetically
into my light.

Jaz

They

They tell her she can't
She'll show them she can
They tell her she "Isn't"
She'll show them she "Is"

They've tried to push her down
She keeps rising
They've tried to hold her back
She keeps coming

You're not good enough
You're not strong enough
You're not smart enough
To them...she's deaf, blind and dumb

But SHE knows she can
SHE knows who she is
SHE is more than good enough
Stronger than they are
Smarter than they'll ever be

SHE is a survivor...and that's something THEY will never understand!

Vee Townsend

The Rest is Silence

I screamed and no one heard
I cried and was ignored
Just like an injured bird
Whose wings no longer soared

I plead to deafen ears
That did not hear a word
In the pain of countless years
No compassion had been stirred

I asked and no one answered
The questions of the heart
The silence was like a cancer
From which I could not depart

Ann Christine Tabaka

A Sham

Don't tell me how to behave
I ain't nobody's slave
At the grand old age of 43
Noone's going to tell me
how to do me
If you don't like my personality
move out of my locality
this is who I am
acting otherwise would be a sham

Susan O'Reilly

Micro-aggression is…

A mute vicious dog
a music-less saxophonist
blowing snapping
a new and un-ignorable
rhythm.

J. Mulcahy-King

Motherly Love

I have spent a lifetime
trying to break away,
trying to break out,
trying to find myself.
Always on the edge,
always on the outside,
not quite a part,
of it, not quite
a beatnik,
or a mod,
hippy, or punk.

I was early to realize that
what she wanted me to be
was what she had wanted
for herself, about her, not me.
I wanted to escape such love.
I thought I could escape.
I thought I had escaped.
And I did, surely I did
Escape some of it.

But not all.
Not enough.
So even now I feel tethered.
After all this time of leaving
her behind,
I remain unsure
of my own.

Lynn White
First published in Yellow Chair Review, June 2016

My Handicap

My handicap does not define me I am not a monster,
No need to be afraid of me

You do not have to whisper
You do not have to even point and stare
Speak to me I dare
I promise you, I will not bite

I am stronger than you think if Just get to know me
My handicap does not define me

We could become great friends and not enemies
Let us learn from each other

In addition, inspire those that are in the unknown
Let the world know they don't have to be afraid,

That being handicap does not define you

Tammy S. Thomas

Coloured

Why do you classify me
By this name?
Aren't we all
Just the same?

This word has killed
So many dreams
It has plotted against me
With many schemes.

This term has undermined
My healthy intelligence
It has caused me suffering
Through your negligence.

Why am I discriminated against
Because of my colour?
Because of your superiority
We had to suffer.

Bevan Boggenpoel

The Necessities of Dark and Light

Out of dark and light
Comes forth
Power
Intelligence
Poetry
Humility
Logic
Breath
Strength
Sarcasm
Charisma
Diversity
Reason
Dissidence
Love
And life itself
These are the beginnings
Of our eternal arrival
These are the necessities
Of our continued survival

John Walker

Vanishing Gardens

The plight of workers in developing nations is often marked with grave injustices. Left without government intervention, workers must seek to survive by working in unimaginable conditions. Such is the condition for this poem's setting. This poem speaks of ongoing conditions found within West Bengal's tea estates. With speculative owners and weak government enforcement of India's Plantation Labor Act, thousands of workers are left destitute and starving to death. While we, as readers, may be removed from such devastating conditions, we share in our responsibility to be our brother's keeper.

Vanishing gardens of West Bengal
your crop's delight are sipped by all
India's finest to offer as tea perfume
savory tea with a lingering scent.

Withering corpses, stand to till your soil
as speculative owners, fatten their vaults
these owners have grafted from land and laborer
leaving shells of both, without any matter.

Indifferent government, turns a blind eye
workers now scurry, hoping not to die
perhaps to mine stones amongst dry river beds
or maybe yet, into human traffic be led?

What can allow a heartless government
to rob a people of their pulse?
while business plunders all human worth
a desert grows of endless thirst.

Baidha Fercoq

Words

Many times
Have words cut deep
Wounding my heart
Slicing my self-esteem
Often words have been
Murderous
Spoken with ignorance
Words describe
What is in need
What is seen
They are reasons for tears
Explanation of fears
Words ignite like fire
Spin webs of liars
Spoken soft with desire
Spoken in trust
Buried with dust
Words can heal
But also steal
They can be warm
Cold or strong
A word spoken
A word written
No matter the creed
It is not forbidden
Words can be enlightening
Words can be inspiring
Fighting and biting
Productive or destructive
My favorite are hers
Very seductive
Progressive not obsessive
Even in silence a word is heard

In a kiss from a heart
Unspoken in her eyes
Read in verse and rhymes
On her lips
Even by blind fingertips

Markus Fleischmann

Mansplain

(From a queer male)

Soap box mansplaination
of phallic proportions
Spitting objective rhetoric
faster than lightning strikes
root
Lack of empathy manifested
in constant back-talk and talking
over
Micro-aggression coffee stains
inhabit his pale-white shirt
While he rambles on and on
about how his views matter more.

Adam Levon Brown

Stressing

Maybe they were right
no one could ever really love me
I'm not like everyone else
I learned early I had to speak up for myself
otherwise people try to break you down to nothing
and hope you can't find any strength left to catch a second breath
yet I must explore the reasons my stress remains distressed
constantly in a state of unrest I wish I could digress
the needles keep pricking me constantly
I don't have any more room for bandages but they aren't listening to me
some of the cuts run deep and were infected by other things
still no one will let me heal
when did this become part of fair deal
if this is reality it surely doesn't seem real
they turned my dreams into nightmares pretending to care
when someone was needed no one was there
or they went deaf and were unable to hear
being alone doesn't always feel so lonely
or have I accepted all of what some have always told me.

Veronica "Vee" Thornton

Heart's Reflection

My reflection is dim and jaded
Unfinished goals sit weak and still
This heart beats numb and faded
How did my dreams used to feel?
I'm struggling to let brokenness go
To renew my peace and my mind.
New growth is desperate to flow
Life is too short to stop and rewind.
Beauty awakens from deep inside
To leave my painful past behind.
There are no more reasons to hide
My heart's success is all in the mind.

Shelly Ambrose

So Pretty

Your make-up looks wonderful!
A comment on a picture
In which I was wearing
Very little make-up

Many people commented
Only this comment
I found not complimentary
It really set my day off badly

I even asked my mom
In case I was being over sensitive
But she and my best friend
Agreed it was rude

That was not the end
They felt the need to message me
No wonder you have a man
Those red lips, who does your make-up?

Because honestly how could I
Get a man otherwise
How could I look so pretty?
Without someone else helping me

I did not post the picture
To get compliments however
Backhanded compliments
Simply show your ugly heart

Maggie Mae

The War Cry of Natives

There's a new wave of huddled masses
Streaming through our ports
Strangers, who bear the full weight of our fears

"Drive them away"
Is the war-cry of so-called natives
From the sons and daughters of old travelers

"Terrorist"
Is scrawled over every proud name
Every doctor, every teacher, every wide-eyed poet
Who dreams and wades into refuge

"Terrorist" is far too small of a word
For the large hearts and minds
Who know, of terror's full wrath

William Wright, Jr.

Embarrassment

Turning red in the face,
heart and nerves fluttering inside,
looking down at my hands,
picking my fingernails and knuckles—
this was my daily routine—
an endless humiliation I
have yet to conquer—

I still feel the pangs,
I still have the dreams,
I still suffer this generation.

Heath Brougher

Personal

You take things too personal
I was just kidding
Really then
Why does it hurt so much?

Shelly Buttenhoff Miller

Collateral Damage

The best of intentions may go haywire
The best of friends may turn into foes
Bunches of bananas may rot with time
And, sometimes, result in collateral damage

In the USA, they were called negro
Then they were called blacks
And, now they are called Afro-Americans
The stigma still sticks to them

Inhabitants of Arctic and sub-Arctic region
Were called Eskimos or 'eaters of raw meat'
Since they took offence, they are called Inuits
Not much has changed beyond their name

Mahatma Gandhi called the despised
Ranks of Indian society 'Harijans'
That means 'People of God'
And, was meant to uplift their lot

Perhaps all these were intended
To improve the lot of these people
And offer them respectable identities
But, they ended up in discrimination

Sometimes things done in good faith
And, best of intentions turn sour
Sometimes efforts to help others
Result in micro-aggression

Vincent Van Ross

Final Depressive Episode

The pain of life is too much to bear, like standing in a
window of a towering inferno
When the heat gets too hot, you jump
That's what happens when you get power, you lose it

Darrell Herbert

In All Walks of Life

Speak when spoken too, isn't this often said
Growing up as a child; as we were being, fed.
But it's much the same, in the grown up world
Especially at work, when you want to get heard.
Those put-downs, insults you feared to answer.
From bullies that have reached places of power
People take advantage in all walks of life
They're not just divisive, their goals to deprive.

Belittle and control others, sometimes subtle,
Unintentional or not, there's always a rebuttal
They'll marginalize you, like an orphan child
Their cruel discriminations make you reviled
Don't buck the trend or you'll not have a friend.
And your stock will fall and forever descend
Speak when spoken too, isn't this often said
Growing into a man and getting, marginally ahead.

Our voices are squashed, in a vice-like-grip
Don't paraphrase them, or their evil editorship
Step back into line or I'll, have you whipped
Locked, behind, bars deported and shipped.
Their racism is trivialized and made the norm
Their doctrine is to lead and thereon… misinform
Wherever you look, there is one unbearable fact
When banded together they are the largest pact.

Mark Andrew Heathcote

Microaggression: A Fabricated Reality

Microaggression
A microcosm
Of absurdity
Of hilarity
A rejection of reality
An acceptance of frailty
A submission to the fealty
Of your limited perspicacity

Xavier Smith

Mirror of Hope

Woke up this morning
With the voice's whispers in my ears
Led me to that mirror

I saw humans
Brothers and sisters
I saw the wars everywhere

I saw the strong eating the weak
I saw friend betrays his friend
And I saw racism still stand tall between us
Terrorists menacing everywhere

Where is the bright future for us?

I'm not the messenger
I'm not an angel
I'm not perfect

I'm just a human who feels the taste of defeat
Tries to change the situation through that faint voice

I look like a blind who walks in daylight
Policy made us enemies.

And we forgot
We are from one race
Humans, brothers and sisters

I wonder where did the white dove go?

Monsif Beroual

The Warrior Takes Her Place

How dare you keep me silent
How dare you take my choice
How dare you abuse and mistreat me
How could you steal my voice!

It's taken me forever
To break out of that spell
Year after year of pain and fear
Locked deep inside your Hell.

Those nightmare days are over
No longer in your grasp
I am no longer silent
I've found my voice at last!

The day I walked away from you
Was my Independence Day
I'm older and much wiser
I've finally found my way

The old life now is over
The new life has begun
No longer trapped in darkness
I've stepped into the Sun

You thought you had me broken
You thought I'd never tell
But that just goes to show you

You did not know me well

That little girl you terrorized
No longer fills my space
And woman stands where once she stood
A warrior took her place!

Vee Townsend

Broken

I opened my heart
To let you in
I bared my soul
Was that my sin

Now I am closed
No more to share
A lesson learned
It hurts to care

Ann Christine Tabaka

My Worst Enemy

My enemy despises me
way too harsh, always critical
quick to judge
unwilling to be any other way

My enemy only see's the ugliness
can't see past the imperfections
won't recognize the beauty
can't acknowledge the good

My enemy finds faults easily
the scars, the weakness in me
too scared to be brave
too fat, no talents

Year after year
I struggled daily
fought so damn hard
only to realize one simple truth
...My enemy is ME!!!

Vee Townsend

Between the Eyes

Without mentioning it, they said it with their words.
They meant it
The subtle hint of cynicism behind facades of altruism
The words, gestures, reactions barge in without a single hint of what's about to happen
Entertaining suggestions of possible deceptions, deciphering, we travel

Body language attacking
Jabbing left and right
Sigh, moan in wonder
Scoff
No explanation
Fingers snapping, tapping
Nails are scratching at the rhythm of the lunatic imagining it all
It's in the eyes of a beast
That won't skip just one feast
to save his dish from suffering
"What's one more day?" he was known to say
and in much the same way ate their judgement away
Suggested situations and scenarios knew no end
Finding enemies in even the closest of friends
For who would judge a friend and what friend would pretend?
Mean cycles, no ends
The unmentioned breaking of the invisible thread
no one knows if it's real
No one knows what just happened
But unless a suggestion of clarity comes
It'll end in all their shend
I won't say it again: it could end

In rumors, accusations, or silence mirroring the rejection of our friends
OR
We can lend them our lens and use theirs when we have it
It might take but a minute to grow understanding
OR
Take it to the depths of the abyss
Where there's no hope of heaven or bliss

Miriam Ruano

This is a Choice

You say this is a choice.
You say that it's a fad that comes and goes.
The reality of this simple idea and thought that fills my soul.
It's nothing more than a play to you.
A performance that can be ended or stopped at anytime.
But my being is overflowing with this one simple fact.
I love him.

I love him in ways that I never knew were real.
His existence fills me with peace and hope and yet that isn't enough.
My mind is a warzone to you.
A place where confusion finds solace and sin is miraged, covered by cloth, hiding itself from me.
If only I were enough.
If only I hadn't turned out this way, then maybe we would both have peace.
But we can't and we won't.

You see, I am confident in my choice.
Not my choice of attraction or disobedience,
But my choice of loving, my choice of him.
If only you could see the words you use as I do.
Simple phrases meant to do good but that are oozing with poison only I can feel.
The sulphuric stench of those words fill my nostrils as I try to understand,
As I try to see through the veil to feel as if I were enough.

You disagree and I do too.
Why talk the talk of love when your actions speak words of unacceptance.

How can you love, yet condemn that same feeling and emotion.
As if we were magnets, you seem to repel while trying to attract.
The pull is strong but the push is stronger.
I don't know where I stand when those words spill out of your mouth.
That it's hard for you and you don't understand.

Then listen.
Hear my heart as it cries out for him.
Hear my soul as it rejoices that I finally want to live.
Feel the vibrations of my words as they sing his praise and all that he's done.
May you never feel this way, torn between two worlds.
Split in half by the prospect that the ones you love may never meet.
That they may never embrace.

Why shy away from a gift when the gift is good.
The tides may change and the wind may shift but I am still me, I am your son.
I am all that you raised me to be and so much more.
There is goodness and light in my actions and words.
Light that shines on everyone I meet, singing on behalf of you.
And yet this is a choice, this is a sin.
These words tear and bruise in ways you can't see or know.

This is choice.
And right now I choose him.

Ezekiel O Tracy

Leper Apothecary

Micro-aggressor
Tells it how it is
educating it with his
leper apothecary
flapping his judgements and
marred reflections
guided by conditioned moral
automaticity
expressed in neurological
ticks
not principles
but older
evolutionary slower
brain snaps
this is how morality moves
but he is unmoving
his apothecary then
is a new kind
of apotheosis
he transforms emotion
into opinion and it shows
he is like me
without the
over-educated
bias but equally
subject to
identity poleis.

J. Mulcahy-King

Promotion

She was extremely pleased
and proud that she reached the
position of senior accountant
Years of hard work and study
finally worked out
Warmly congratulated by
her co-workers,
flooded by compliments
Though, she couldn't ignore
the whispers behind her back
'only got promoted cause
 she fucked the boss'
When she got a hold
of these words, she smiled
She never fucked the boss
but a simple blowjob
has truly upgraded her income

Daginne Aignend

Nation in Reparation

Our broken society
Must take priority
For too long we've been
The innocent enemy.

Mending the pieces
That was ripped apart
By a system
With a stone cold heart.

It has caused unbearable pain
And much decay
But our social unity
Well on its way.

We've managed to claim back
That which was stolen
By an apartheid system
Which now has fallen.

Our dignity, culture
Religion and pride
Can no longer
Be brushed aside.

A nation united
In reparation
We have eliminated
The segregation invasion.

Bevan Boggenpoel

The F*cking Bus Seat Saga

My crammed bag manages to
squeeze past by the rest of the
passengers, their eyes catch
mine in their territorial gaze,
As if I shouldn't sit next to them
or they will silently move their
legs away, hoping that I don't
notice. You don't own that f*cking
seat, my brain points out, I let
the thought pass by – why are
we territorial over things that we
don't own? Why do we shy away from
things that are unknown?
Our sense of order is owned by
the bus seat. Tied to the material,
the proud decorative owner,
Once your ass heats the seat up,
you'll leave your owner's warmth
as you leave at the next bus stop,
You'll clamber off like a penguin on
a slippery bowling alley, waddling away
from your beloved seat.
Instantly, I move and sit in your seat.
Now, it's my f*cking seat.

Zoe Maynard

Black Smells

It all started with Dicky
When Jesse entered a classroom
Dicky began to sniff loudly,
looked as if he smelled
something revolting, and declaimed
'What a disgusting reek over here,
Oh, that must be Jesse, burned black'
Since then, Jesse was haunted by
sniffing, snorting and sniggering
giggling behind his back
Even Roslyn, who was always
so kind, avoided him
He lost his appetite, his lust for life,
being the eternal laughing-stock
at school

Does the pitch-dark color
of his skin make him
a lesser human being?
Jesse drowned in his
own insecurity, doubts
and hopelessness
They found him,
laying on his bed
A small note clutched
in his hand
'Sorry, I can't go on!
Please, don't cremate me'

Daginne Aignend

Subtle Aggression

I was deeply hurt -
By your subtle remark
It resounds in my head -
Like a dog's bark

It ripped apart -
My caring heart
It left a stench -
Like a skunk's fart

You might have done it -
Unintentionally
But it affected me -
Mentally

I feel like a car accident -
A wreck
I always thought -
You had my back

My best friend -
I trusted the most
Has burned my soul -
Like a chicken for roast

Bevan Boggenpoel

Whistle

It was his fault.

No awareness of personal space.
He shoved past me, brushing
my handbag with his suit, a phone
held to his ear.

Sweat ran down my forehead,
down my cheeks, and left
streak marks that ruined my
face of make-up.

My nylon tights had ripped
slightly by the seam, I tried
to hide the exposed skin,
though, the hole enlarged.

Damn it.

Drilling sounds dug through my
ear canals, sailing into my brain,
I ripped out my headphones, the aggressive
drilling overpowered the acoustics.

The sky started to spit rain
towards the ground. I crossed the
road, avoiding the drilling disruption,
and heard one of the workers
wolf-whistle at me.

Time wasn't on my side, five minutes
to get to work. I curled the sides of my
mouth upwards, faking a smile

at his intimidation.

Why should I feel intimidated?

I then held up my middle finger
in the air, his eyes stared back at me
in shock, mouth open.

The angry lioness within me overruled
my patience. I felt empowered
and alive.

Zoe Maynard

Swept Aside

Sometimes it may feel as if our life's efforts are insignificant; silently consigned to meaningless routines. This poem offers another perspective by suggesting the most unnoticed and unsought activities often spring from the most noble and highest callings of service to humanity.

You thought you were swept aside
by eyes that sought to avert your gaze
you thought your life was minimized
by value, society placed upon your wage.

For untold years, you swept the streets
amongst the trash, others tossed and threw
in silence you toiled with smile on face
your poor self-worth, it never grew.

At day's long end
when slumber you seek
you mind should know
tis not you, society does dread.

Society has put on a cloak
to shield itself from man's greater worth
for it is you, in your lowly tasks
reminding man of a rising truth.

A true worth of man is found
not within the wage he earns
but simply upon
the call of which, his heart does yearn.

Baidha Fercoq

Let Go

Your vibration of negativity
Suffocates my dreams
Take a few steps back
I'm about to scream
Then fly-
Don't get dust in your eyes
Maybe blinded,
Your heart will clearly see
Your abandoned dreams
Just let mine be!

Shelly Ambrose

Raised On Cartoons

Tom and Jerry were the focus
of my pre-adolescent life in the early mornings eating breakfast
in the living room yet somehow never seeing blood.
That mouse pulled that cat's tongue out
and then fed him to the dog.

In my youth, the mouse would blow up the cat
with giant proportions of dynamite and bombs.
In adulthood, us kids are still blowing things up.
This time with giant proportions of bombs much stronger
than dynamite.

Nowadays when I try to slip back
into that innocence of pure childhood
it seems like one enormously glowing violent morning after another
all bathed in the bloodied glow of a numb haze.

The insides reek like a stale mind's acrid scent.
Intestinally heartless—a carcass once was mine—
must I remind you of the blood drenched grass
and tears that smeared the world like a giant stain?

Heath Brougher

Who Are You?

Are you the . . .

Enforcer
the
Loyal
the
Whore
the
Victim
the
Alcoholic
the
Comedian
the
Addict
the
Free Spirit
the
Activist
the
Follower

Who Are You?

Who do you allow yourself to be?

Paige Turner

The Micro Female

How does my blond pigment
measure my intelligence?
"Dumb blond," before I open
my mouth; your disappointment
at not keeping up with my
vernacular, my vocabulary,
your joke was wasted on me.

When did large breasts deem me
"easy pickings," my physicality
inviting cheap cat calls, sleazy
come on lines; your visible
disappointment when you
underestimated my morality;
your attentions wasted on me

Why does my gender equate
to weakness, my genitalia
mysteriously connoting an
ineptitude of being informed,
incapable of critical thinking,
incapable of leadership, spoken
to with subtle condescension

Assumptions, I dare say, is the
bane of an awakened society.

Brenda-Lee Ranta

Diary of a Coloured Boy

The Train Journey

Today is my first train journey into Cape Town City with my sister, Ruth. I grew up with the sight of majestic Table Mountain towering above the city and indeed, visible from the whole region around the city and the distant escarpment mountains and the Atlantic seaboard; like a blue stone centurion guarding the mother city, watching, protecting a divided nation. Ruth promised me that on my tenth birthday that she would take me into the city to celebrate my big day. Although the apartheid boards for 'whites only' were removed from first class train carriages, beaches, benches, buses, restaurants etc., most of us who were branded under South African law as 'coloured' still kept to ourselves, interacted with our kind and still sat in third class train carriages. I'm just glad I was brought up to respect anyone, despite their colour, culture or religion. I can see the mountain looming above now. I can hardly contain my excitement, as I was promised a ride with the cable car to go up Table Mountain. At least we were allowed to! The train slowly came to a stop as we arrived in the 'coloureds and blacks only' side of the central station, as nothing has really changed. I saw a blonde girl wave at me and I naturally waved back with a huge smile but then I saw her mother shouting at her and her smile evaporated. I could not understand what I did wrong, as her mother glared at my sister and I with piercing, accusatory eyes. I was very confused but my sister just gripped my hand more tightly.

Don Beukes

Uncomfortable Question

As a classroom of students prepared for an exam, a white student turned to an Asian student and asked, "Dude, will you solve this problem for me? It's really hard but I know you can solve it." The Asian student agreed to help the White student but couldn't help but feel uncomfortable with the way the question was asked. The rest of the day the Asian student wondered.... Did he know I could solve the problem because I'm smart? Or because we're friends? Or because I'm Asian.

John Walker

Monks Swimming

"In the name of god there are no monks swimming!"
Father Flynn slammed the desk with his prayer book. And Michael Rooney woke up with a jolt. The priest eyed him.
"What should it be Rooney?"
Rooney's milk-face went traffic-light red under the crop of his amber hair.
"Stand up when I'm speaking - you little, ginger Gobshite!"
Father Flynn flashed a look about, to make sure Mr. Jarvis wasn't there and that he wasn't overheard.
"Monks praying..." stammered Rooney.
"Jesus, Mary and Joseph what have I done to deserve the lot of ye! Blessed art thou amongst monks praying! Is that it?"
I slouched down behind Theresa O'Dowd. I shut my eyes to become invisible and saw a pool full of swimming monks. Some were drowning, dragged down by their Dominican habits. Roly-poly and black and white, the way I'd seen in a film of penguins.
"You Danny Callaghan...If the priest in confession gives you a penance of a hail Mary. Can you say it?"
I stood up, trying to be smaller than I was. I was visible again.
"Don't slouch boy. Begin! "Father Flynn drummed his fingers on Mr. Jarvis desk.
"...And blessed art thou monks swimming."
Then Father Flynn was upon me and the whack about my head sent me flying all over the lovely Theresa O'Dowd...Little black flecks flashed across my eyes. She screamed, now under me.
"Now get up and say after me..." Father Flynn pulled on my collar. "All of you!"
Just then, Mr. Jarvis limped in and Father Flynn turned gentle and removed me off of Theresa, who was making

herself decent again, tugging down her skirt, to hide her navy blue knickers. Father Flynn cast a sort of smile at Mr. Jarvis.

"Mr. Jarvis, we are learning what penance means, and the correct pronunciation of the Hail Mary…" Father Flynn turned to me. I was treading water now, amid the monks, swimming and drowning.

"It should be…and repeat after me…"

"Repeat after me…" the class chanted.

"No the prayer!" He shouted.

"No the prayer!" we shouted back.

"…And blessed art though - amongst! Amongst! Not monks-swimming…amongst women, and blessed is the fruit of thy womb Jesus…"

Word for word we chanted. "…And blessed art though amongst…amongst…not monks swimming…amongst women, and blessed is the fruit of thy womb, Jesus…"

Now I saw apples and cherries, fruit floating between the swimming monks…wondering what a womb was, for it sounded like tomb…

Mr. Jarvis leaned on his walking stick…

"Thank-you Father Flynn, for your help. I will finish the First communion class from here."

I slid back into the darkening water and was floating. Then I was being scooped out of the pool of drowning monks and swirling fruit and Mr. Jarvis was laying me out on the floor in the staff room. Perhaps the rest of the monks had drowned. The fruit was nowhere. Mrs. McCartney the headmistress put a wet cloth on my forehead.

"He'll be fine." Mr. Jarvis said. "I've seen worse." He drew a blanket up to my chin.

"Your dreaming will be the death of you Danny Callaghan.

"He pushed my hair back from my eyes.

"Swimming…fruit…" I mumbled.
"You'll be fine. I need to go back to class." He said. I turned my head as he limped his way to the door. We never mocked him for it. We whispered our stories about it. Once when Theresa was writing a war story, she read the bit where she jumped out of the way of a German bomb…and was praying for help. Mr. Jarvis set into her.
"Good God child! I was two hundred yards from a bomb and I'm only here by the grace of god. And by god we said our Hail Mary's that day…"
The class had gone silent. He just shook his head gently…He tapped on her exercise book. "There's a silent b at the end of bomb- there…"
I remember thinking, how odd that a bomb has a silent letter….
Then, from the classroom I heard, "Hail Mary full of grace, the lord is with thee…blessed at thou amongst woman…"
There were no monk's swimming Mr. Jarvis was praying. I could hear the class praying with him.
"…And blessed is the fruit of thy womb, Jesus. Holy Mary, mother of God pray for us sinners, now and at the hour of our death. Amen.
There was a silent b in womb and tomb. They were long words. Bomb was short. I remember thinking of Grace- a girl's name…soft.
There were no monks swimming any more, when I closed my eyes.

Jim Lewis

Why Am I Angry

The doctor diagnosed me with displaced anger long ago. In grade school, those "bad kids" called me slow! My daddy is a "womanizer" and a "wife beater, and a sperm donor. He places everybody before me! I'm not the one who's angry, I'm not the one with issues. I know exactly where the displacement belongs. It belongs on them. It belongs on all those people who acted like they didn't even know my name. See, I told you I'm not the one to blame for all this pent -up aggression. The golden rule must have been changed. Somebody, somewhere didn't learn that lesson. My momma said, "Baby treat people like you want to be treated". I tried hard, but my emotions so soft they just break! Sometimes I feel so defeated. I can't win, every time I turn around I'm losing friends. Some of them aren't so loyal either! I know, I know… I got to get over this hump somehow. Truth be told, I've been dealing with self-esteem issues sense I was a child. People please have some patience. Take time to look a little deeper! The truth doesn't always lay in some case file or collect dice mice on my case manager's desk. I feel there are no secrets I must confess. Once and for all, let me get this heavy load off my chest! Who's going to lift the weight of my burdens? I don't desire or deserve to wear these various labels of "crazy. "The psychos want me to believe that medication is always the answer. Well, I guess my blank faced stare told them everything they need to know! Don't dare ask me again, how does it feel? I'm the one who's sitting here waiting and wondering why I must endure this! Right now, I have a headache and my heartaches bad. More than just my feet hurt. For a moment, walk in my shoes! Try this one on for size. If forgiveness is for me, not you Why am I angry?

Terika McQuinn

Personal Experience

My friend is African-American and I am European-American. We were leaving a grocery store when we saw an elderly white woman struggling with her groceries. We asked if she needed help and she asked if we could give her a ride home. We said yes and chatted along the way. When we dropped her off and unloaded her bags she was very thankful. She looked at my friend and said. "You black people sure got a lot better when you finally got some of that good old slave owner white blood in you." My friend bowed her head, sighed then shook it off. She felt sorry for the lady. We drove away.

John Walker

Words Can Hurt

I was only 13 years old when I came to America from Germany and far too often was made to feel like an outsider, someone who didn't belong. I remember a time in 8th grade during history class when we had the subject about WWII and the question was who were the Axis and Allies. None of my peers knew the difference and when I answered with my broken English a student answered, "Of course the Nazi would know". That was one of many remarks made and it didn't stop. Later in life as I grew up living in America, I encountered many "racial" remarks. Why is that? Is being different so bad? Why do we need to stereotype in this society? It is wrong to say that all Hispanics are 'dirty', that blacks are 'criminals', or that Chinese are 'taking over the country'. We are all equal. No matter what our race or religion is, we have the right to be respected for who we are. To grow, to be unique in our own greatness and intelligence and we should never be made to feel different by stereotypes and racist comments. Words hurt and they do damage to a person's self-esteem. Those wounds don't easily heal and often they leave a scar that will keep that person from going the extra mile. I know; I'm one of them. I hated how I was growing up. There were many times I wished I was born American so I could fit in and not feel like I was this alien nobody liked.

Words can hurt, words can wound.
Words can manifest and fester deep within.
It need not be this way, for we are all human; brothers, sisters
- kin.

Markus Fleischmann

The Restaurant

After the weird incident with that strange white lady in the main arrival hall at Cape Town central, my sister just told me to ignore it and to enjoy the rest of the day. She dragged me into a pie shop to buy my favourite steak and kidney 'Big Jack' pie and a Schweppes lemon twist fizzy drink before taking the minibus from Adderley Street up to Kloofnek, where we had to take the shuttle higher up to reach the cable way station. I was so excited, I spilled my drink as I stared down to the 'mother city' below as Cape Town was affectionately known, for me the most beautiful city in the world.

We lined up to take the next cable car. I was mesmerized by this futuristic shape floating down towards us. As we ascended, I thought I was dreaming, as it whisked us upwards into the heavens, rising one thousand meters above sea level. The strange thing was that we were the only 'coloureds' in that cable car and to my surprise the blonde girl from the station was staring right at me! She waved again but this time her family was with her and they all turned their backs on us, muttering under their breaths of our audacity to be in the same space as them. I wonder if they ever knew how that felt? It did not feel nice at all.

Anyway, after the spectacular views, Ruth decided to take me to the fancy restaurant there. As soon as we entered, a man rushed to the door and asked with a raised voice in Afrikaans, 'Ja, kan ek julle help?' meaning 'Yes, can I help you?' I thought he was very rude. My sister politely asked for a table near the window and he reluctantly took us to one, whilst muttering under his breath. When the waitress arrived, she almost threw the eating utensils down on the table and half shouted 'Wat wil julle bestel?' meaning 'What do you want to order?' I looked at my sister and asked her why the people here were so rude to us. She just smiled weakly and told me to enjoy the amazing views but I could see the familiar pain clouding her eyes. I thought there must be something wrong with us. I would find out myself a couple of years later...

Don Beukes

Coco Sonya

I have a wonderful, longtime friend named Sonya. She is one of the most beautiful people I've ever met, both physically and in personality. On a gorgeous Sunday we had lunch at a fast food chicken place. After she had ordered her grilled chicken sandwich, she looked to me and said, "Black people have to watch what they eat, because it will go right to our butt". I couldn't help but smile, the reason being she is always transparent with me. That is one of the best compliments a person can pay.

Rusty Shuping

Good Deeds that Turn Out the Other Way

I have a woman journalist friend I take for a daughter. Once someone asked her if there is a possibility of a good story being done for her newspaper. The request was well-meaning and the story was a genuine human interest story.

My daughter was about to say 'Yes' when a photographer friend intervened. He thought that she can only write and submit the story but had no real say over whether or not it would be published. To save her from embarrassment, he countered: 'She is only a journalist. She is not the owner of the newspaper. She can only write the story. But, she cannot ensure that your story gets into the newspaper.' Actually, she had done many such stories and they were carried by the newspaper. Only once in a while they spiked her story here and there. There was every chance that this story would have found the necessary space in the newspaper and carried in the next edition of the newspaper. But, his interjection prevented that from happening. The photographer might have been trying to protect the journalist's interest but she felt insulted. In other words, his intervention resulted in micro-aggression.

Vincent Van Ross

Luck or Blessing

While traveling in Western Kenya our small white van was bumping along on the narrow dirt road. I could see ahead some girls walking home from school. They spotted me right away and began yelling Muzungu, Muzungu, with much enthusiasm. The van was moving slowly and the girls reached out into the road toward the vehicle. As we passed by I was able to high five a few. I could hear their giggles of excitement for two reasons. The first being they were exceptionally friendly. Secondly there was the rural legend that if they touched a white person it would bring good luck. I am not so sure about me bringing the luck thing but they were a blessing to me making me feel welcome.

Rusty Shuping

Things I have Heard Said

He/she has learning disabilities
"Please" direct your questions to me.

Those people are, really tiny & cute!
Look they're like Santa's little helpers.

"God knows we tried & tried & tried"
Teenagers eh, who'd have them?

I've bent over backwards for them people
"Do I get any, kind of god damn thanks?"
No, none whatsoever? Bloody foreigners!

Mark Andrew Heathcote

The Beach

In my late teens, I looked forward to return to our favourite holiday destination on the south coast, called Struisbaai, located near the most southern tip of the African continent, Cape Agulhas. We stayed in the only camping site for 'coloureds' or mixed race people, as whites still had their own resort further up the coast with fancy chalets and facilities closer to the town. One day all my cousins and some new friends, girls and boys decided as a group to do the unthinkable and walk to the beach, which was still unofficially reserved for whites. We have never done this before and looked forward to mingle with teenagers on that side. Just to put it into perspective, this was about three years before the first democratic elections were held in a racially divided South Africa. As we got closer, we were determined to act normal and decided to just wade into the water and splash about like normal teenagers would do when on holiday. We became aware of some holiday makers speedily making their way to where we were frolicking about. Some burly red faced men with sunburnt beer bellies started shouting at us to get out of the water. One waved frantically to us to turn back and threatened us to turn around and to go back to where we came from. We just all laughed at the spectacle and continued walking closer to their camp and some of us took another quick dip. Suddenly the whole beach was a hive of activity . One older lady pointed a bony finger at us and shrieked from the top of her voice, 'Wat soek hulle hier op ons strand?' meaning 'What are they doing here at our beach?' Another lady shouted for the police and insisted for them to escort us back to where we came from. Although we pretended to laugh and make light of the situation, we knew that we disturbed a hornet's nest but also realised we had to do it to find out for ourselves. As we were accompanied back to our beach, I sensed one of the policemen slightly nudging his snarling police dog closer to us because we did not line up with the group. When they eventually let us walk freely, one of my more daring cousins dropped his pants to one of the policemen and did some crazy dance. We all burst out laughing, even though one of the dogs were let loose but it was called back at the last moment. We just felt that we at least achieved something and felt a little bit braver about the future. The same water we swam in they swam in, the same air we breathed they breathed and the same sun beating down on us shone at them. At least we were happy and was able to travel around freely but just not in areas where we were not welcome, not yet. We did not hate them for it, just confused about why they hated us so much...

Don Beukes

It's all Perspective

In 1968 North Carolina may have been a little behind as far as desegregation goes a new school year was here, in the seventh grade and only a few days into it. I was taking everything in with the appetite for knowledge that comes with being a boy. I loved to be able to time in my grandpa's shop where he sharpened saws and other tools for the public. On a certain late summer day, one of the men in the shop broke away from the regular "bull", looked to me and asked. "What do you think about going to school with black people"? Now mind you I had to this point never had any close contact with black people. I had to think for a few seconds and then replied as truthful as I could be, "I don't know, but they all look alike to me". This was the new perspective of a 13 year old boy living in the South.

Rusty Shuping

There is No Micro in Aggression

Micro: meaning smaller than the average scale
Aggression: meaning the act of attacking without provocation

Microaggression, although a term coined in 1970, I would argue that it is just an alternate word for "stereo typing," combined with "passive aggression."

I would suggest that openly aggressive behavior existed prior to the 1970's when describing any type of diversity. Humanity has not been kind. The word "cancer" was spoken of in hushed whispers. To say it out loud would invite it unto yourself. To have "epilepsy," which involved brain function, deemed you mentally unfit. To have any type of disability, coined you as "crippled," "deaf and dumb," "mentally retarded." Being of a religion which was not mainstream, meant you were a "cult follower." To marry outside your church, deemed you "ostracized." To marry outside of your race, meant you were of a "mixed marriage." To be homosexual was to be hidden, disgusting and "abnormal." It was unabashed, it was raucous. I will not expound on the ethnic slurs given to define different races or nationalities; our shameful memories recall.

Such phrases and terms marginalized people, stereo typed them; there was such a negative connotation attached, which in itself was highly aggressive. How wonderful it all seemed, yet how naive I was to have actually believed this to be a thing of the past. I would argue now, given the present day geopolitical temperature that either we have spun backwards forty years, or the sleeping dragons have awoken. Religion has legitimized the revival of the latest round of political racist rhetoric. The separation of church and state is non-existent; redefining people based on geography, religious practices, the clothes of their cultures, their sexual preferences, their skin colour and indeed even their gender. There is no room for diversity in the new political box. There is nothing "micro" nor "passive" about this; bigotry, racism, xenophobia and homophobia is alive and well, back out of the dark closet it crawled from.

Thankfully, a clear line in the sand has been drawn. Those of us who know intrinsically that all human beings are of equal value, are sickened and incensed by those who think themselves to be the moral barometer for society, creating divisiveness to gain power, will now have to contend with us. We will not be silent anymore. It is an affront to our awakened nature to have hatred thrust upon us again. We are not cattle, blindly following some maniacal ideology, borne of untruths and manufactured crisis. We refuse to paint all our brothers and sisters with the same can of spray paint; good and bad exists in every culture. White, homogeneous superiority is disgustingly abhorrent to us. The ambiguous Commentary is not lost on us; be us people of colour, be us gay, be us women, be us physically challenged.

I would dare say, we are well past Microaggression. I believe this to be Macroaggression. Subjugation of any human being, based on diversity is sheer evil. It defies the basic human consciousness, in that "we are all innately born good."

I do not subscribe to sympathy; sympathy is for the survivors of the dead. I would dare say empathize, slip your feet into another person's shoes, walk their path within your heart.

See yourself in every person's eyes, in every person's struggle. We are humanity.

I am a woman. I am a writer. I am a human being first. I for one, will not stay silent!

Brenda-Lee Ranta

Publishing Assistance

Starving Artist

In 2013 Ms. Raja Williams realized that there was a gap, a void if you will, within the publishing industry. A writer either had to come up with hundreds, sometimes thousands of dollars to release a book or take on the journey of self-publishing alone. There was no middle ground, no one there to assist, either financially or lead the way in self-publishing. Most writers do not have the finances to pay a publisher, and some don't know where to start when it comes to self-publishing, nor are they prepared to be in business for themselves.

Raja was inspired to start a fund to assist writers in becoming published authors at either a discounted rate or a full publishing scholarship. To begin this fund Raja paid for the publishing of our first anthology *Love, a Four Letter Word*, comprised of poets from all around the world. The sales generated from the purchases of the book were placed into a fund that enabled us to fund future publishings.

We now are able to offer anthology publications, a chance for authors to have a voice in the literary world yearly, and we have been able to offer several authors full scholarships, as well as offering deeply discounted publishing services as a whole. We are thankful for the continued support of this program by both our readers and writers alike.

For More Information Please Visit Our Website At:

www.ctupublishinggroup.com/starving-artist-fund.html

Get Connected With Us!

Website: Creative Talents Unleashed Publishing Group

www.ctupublishinggroup.com

Facebook: Get connected with us on our Facebook Page

www.Facebook.com/Creativetalentsunleashed

Twitter: https://twitter.com/CTUPublishing

Blog: www.creativetalentunleashed.com

Pinterest: https://www.pinterest.com/creativetalents/

Instagram: https://instagram.com/ctupublishinggroup/

Creative Talents Unleashed

Creative Talents Unleashed is an independent publishing group that offers writers an opportunity to share their writing talents with the world. We are committed to fostering and honoring the work of writers of all cultures. Our publishing group offers writing tips to assist writers in continued growth and learning, daily writing prompts and challenges to keep the writers mind sharp and challenged, marketing and events, as well as a variety of yearly publishing opportunities. We are honored to be assisting writers in the journey of becoming published authors.

www.ctupublishinggroup.com

For More Information Contact:

Creativetalentsunleashed@aol.com

www.ingramcontent.com/pod-product-compliance
Lightning Source LLC
Chambersburg PA
CBHW071323040426
42444CB00009B/2070